CARTOON FUNdamentals

DICK EVANS

ISBN: 978-0-9798363-1-2

Printed in the United States of America
10 9 8 7 6 5 4 3 2 1

www.bearclausepublications.com

A Note From the Author

How many times have you wanted to capture a funny situation on paper, but were stumped by the thought of drawing?

Now you can learn to create your own cartoons and caricatures with this easy-to-follow program that shows you how to draw one step at a time.

The basic premise of *Cartoon FUNdamentals* is: **"You can't do it wrong!"** Your art is a personal expression of how you view the world. Therefore, *what you draw is right for you.* This method encourages self-esteem and self-expression. Everyone draws in his or her unique way— this is good . . . *not* wrong!

Many adults and children are threatened by the mere idea of drawing. Life experience has programmed them to view *different* as *wrong*. Thus, they are unwilling to try cartooning.

After working with hundreds of people, I know that by building your skill through practice, practice, and practice your confidence will increase with each sketch. Embrace the you-can't-do-it-wrong philosophy and become free from the fear of failure.

If you are helping someone use this booklet, please respect the above principles. If you see something another way, draw it that way for yourself. Celebrate the unique creativity of all individuals. Emphasize self-expression. Learn from it.

So, what are you waiting for? Grab some paper and a pencil and get started! Remember: You CAN'T do this wrong.

Tips to Improve Your Drawing

- **Remember the rule:** You can't do it wrong. Don't worry about what others think. If you like it . . . it is right!

- **Draw quickly.** Let the pencil flow. Let your instincts guide you.

- **Draw with a pencil.** Erasers are an artist's best friend. Once you have drawn it the way you like it, then you can go over it with a pen to make it permanent.

- **Exaggerate** size and/or features for a more dramatic effect.

- **Experiment.** Try something new. Start with any feature. Start with the nose or hair. Draw "outside the box."

- **Mix and Match.** Use a combination of different ears, eyes, etc. Create your own style.

- **Teach.** You will learn faster by teaching and listening to others. Two (or more) heads *are* better than one, especially in creative endeavors.

- **Relax.** Enjoy yourself. This is supposed to be FUN!

STEP 1: HEAD

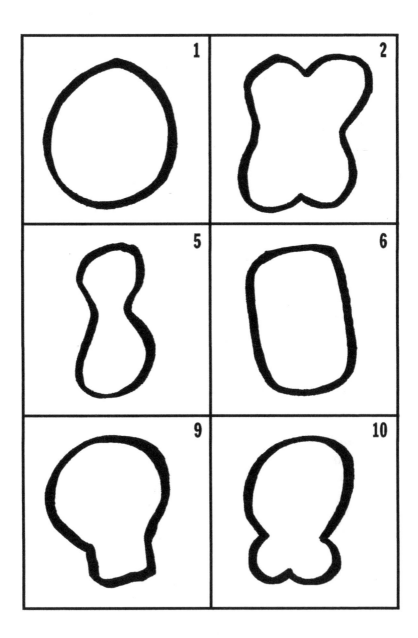

STEP 1: HEAD

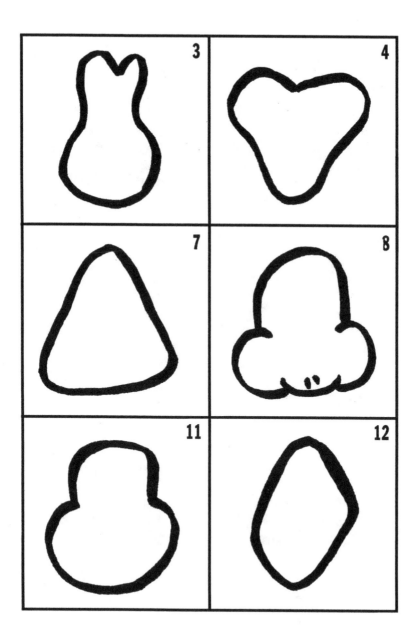

STEP 2: EYES

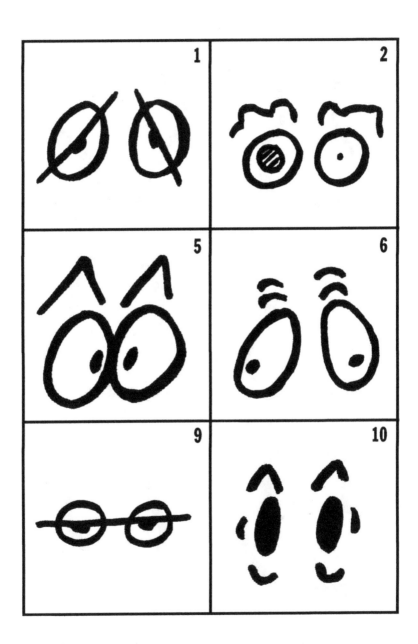

STEP 2: EYES

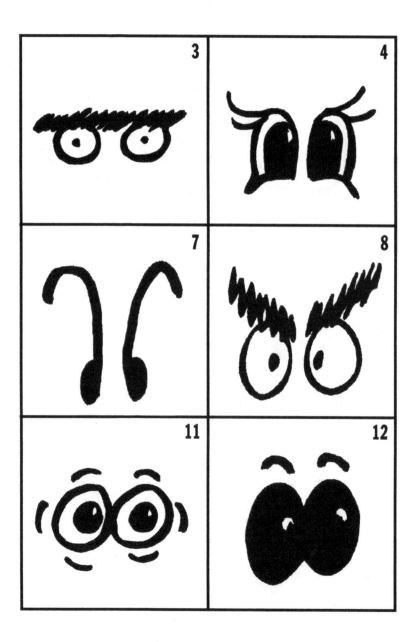

STEP 3: NOSE

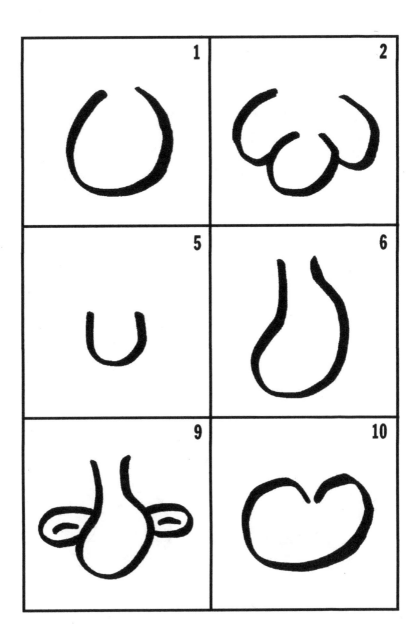

STEP 3: NOSE

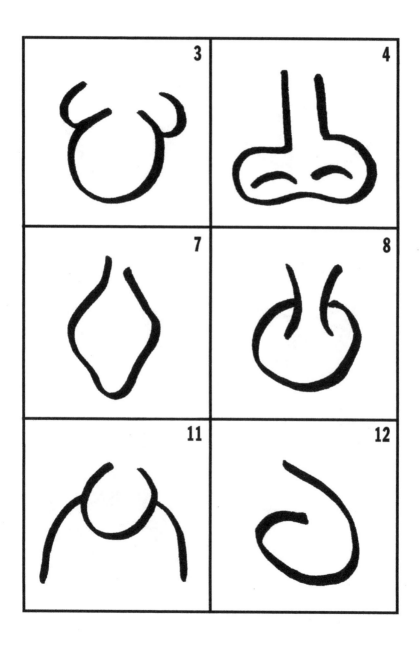

STEP 4: MOUTH

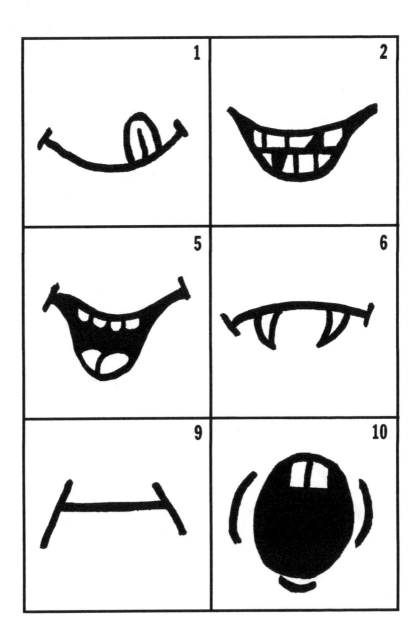

STEP 4: MOUTH

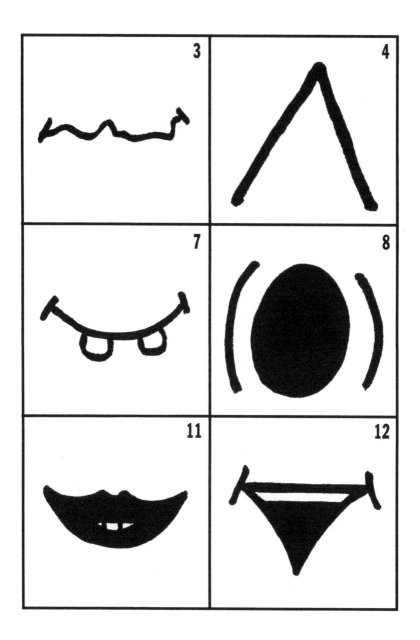

STEP 5: EARS

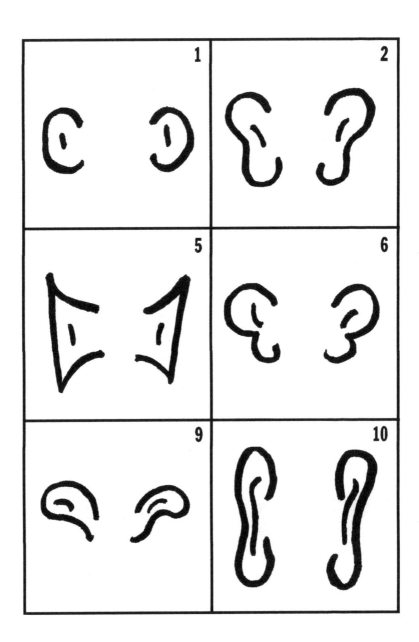

STEP 5: EARS

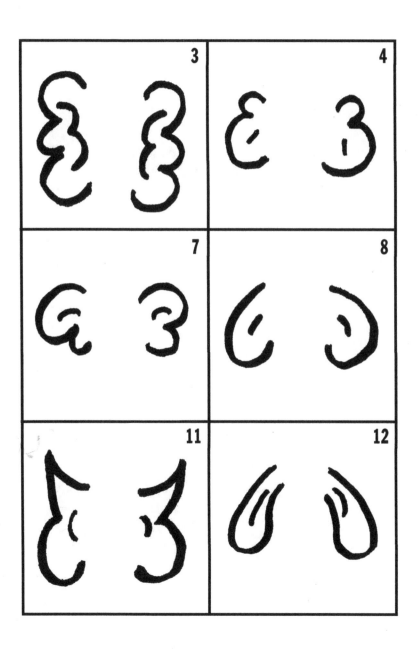

STEP 6: HAIR

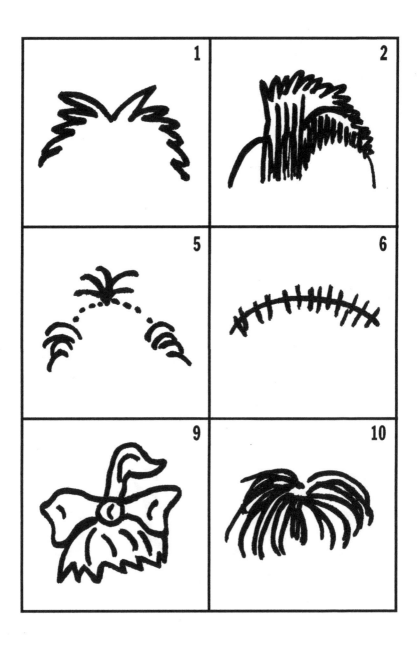

STEP 6: HAIR

STEP 7: NECK

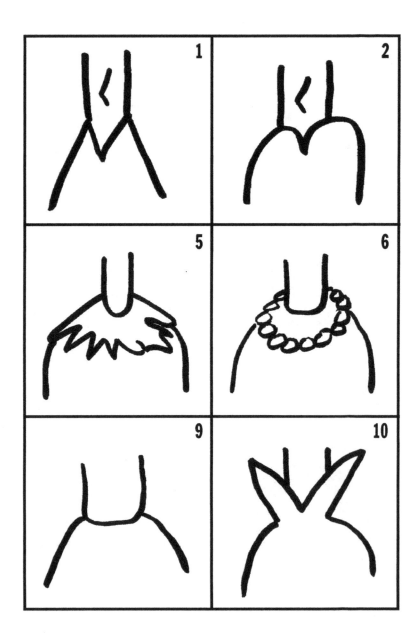

STEP 7: NECK

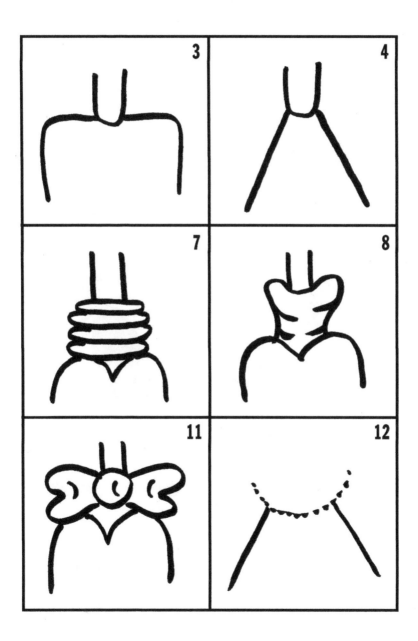

STEP 8: EXTRAS

Glasses 1	Mustache 2
Stitches 5	Beanie 6
Baseball Hat 9	Heavy Eyebrows 10 & Mustache

STEP 8: EXTRAS

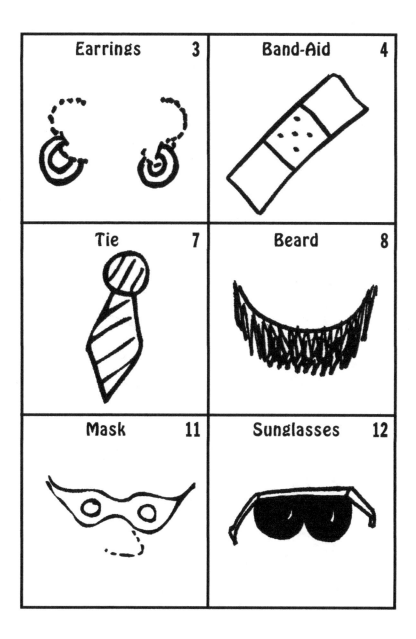

STEP 9: STICK FIGURES

Running 1

Walking 2

Bowling 5

Tennis 6

Hockey 9

Snowboarding 10

STEP 9: STICK FIGURES

STEP 10: BODY

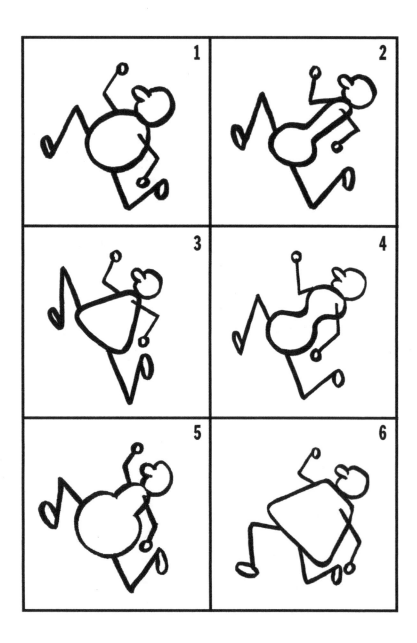

STEP 11: PUTTING IT TOGETHER

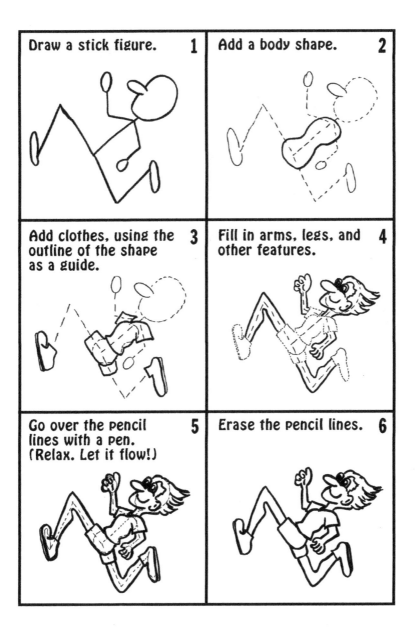

Draw a stick figure. 1

Add a body shape. 2

Add clothes, using the outline of the shape as a guide. 3

Fill in arms, legs, and other features. 4

Go over the pencil lines with a pen. (Relax. Let it flow!) 5

Erase the pencil lines. 6

About the Author

Ever since he was a teenager, **DICK EVANS** has combined his artistic talent and quick wit to create humorous cartoons and illustrations. In 1977, he began to share his love of cartooning by becoming a part-time drawing instructor. *Cartoon FUNdamentals* is the result of years of searching to find a simple, non-threatening approach to illustrating.

People of all ages, including adults, have benefited from Dick's instruction. In addition to teaching classes at Northwestern Michigan College in Traverse City, Michigan, he travels to schools and other locations. "Have pen, will travel" is his motto.

Dick focuses on individual creativity and stresses only one classroom rule: You can't do it wrong. He believes everyone has an artist lurking inside him or her that is only waiting to be released.

His work has appeared in numerous local, state, and national publications and Dick is the creator of Tourist Country Bear, a.k.a. TC Bear, who is featured in *UP NORTH with TC Bear*, a coloring book that highlights tourist activities in Northern Michigan.

To inquire about classes and to obtain copies of his publications, contact Dick Evans at **231-943-7689** or visit:

www.bearclausepublications.com